KATIE RODEN

PLAGUE

COPPER BEECH BOOKS
BROOKFIELD, CONNECTICUT

© Aladdin Books Ltd 1996

Designed and produced by
Aladdin Books Ltd
28 Percy Street
London W1P OLD

First published in
the United States in 1996 by
Copper Beech Books,
an imprint of
The Millbrook Press
2 Old New Milford Road
Brookfield, Connecticut 06804

Editors
Sarah Levete, Jim Pipe
Design
David West Children's Book Design
Designer
Flick Killerby
Picture Research
Brooks Krikler Research
Illustrators
Richard Rockwood
Rob Shone

Printed in Belgium
All rights reserved

CIP data is on file at the Library of Congress

ISBN 0-7613-0541-6 (lib. bdg.)
ISBN 0-7613-0516-5 (pbk.)

CONTENTS

PLAGUE

It was the year 2034. The huge orange sun sank gradually in the blood-red sky, its glowing light reflected in the wine-colored waters of the Pacific Ocean.

It was a perfect evening on the island — calm, warm, and still. Or perhaps too still. On an average night the air would be humming with birdsong, the call of animals among the trees, and the chatter of the islanders as they pulled in their fishing nets and watched their children playing in the breakers. But now the only sound was the lapping of the waves, breaking the eerie silence that hung over the island.

As always, the beach was full of people, but tonight their bodies lay still, twisted in agony, their mouths open in silent, tortured screams.

The silence was broken by the whirring of a turbocopter overhead. The pilots looked in horror at the gruesome scene. "My God," whispered the navigator. "What on earth has happened? Quick, turn this thing around and I'll videophone the base." The chopper swung around and sped back to the security of the mainland. Behind the high walls of Alpha City, they would be safe from this invisible terror.

WHAT IS A PLAGUE?

When you think of a plague, what do you see in your mind's eye? Perhaps a wave of flea-bitten rats *(left)*, rushing through the streets of medieval Europe, or grisly images of ancient plagues described in history or legend. Do you wonder why some plagues are a thing of the past?

THE TIMELESS DESTROYER

You're right to think of all these things, as pestilence in its many forms has cursed the human race since history began.

This book charts those terrible plagues, both mythical and horribly real. Discover how humans have battled against the bacteria and viruses which can cause disease *(left)*, from the bizarre treatments of European plague doctors *(right)* to the wonder drugs of the 20th century.

A MODERN TERROR

Plagues can strike, at any time. Fields are wasted by swarms of insects, while mysterious diseases continue to defeat modern medicine. Even in our hi-tech world, the threat of pestilence is ever-present. Who knows what horrors the future holds...?

NO ESCAPE

Even if you go to the movies, you may be plagued by tales of cities devastated by disease or overrun by marauding insects. In the 1956 film *Them!*, a colony of giant radioactive ants terrorized the citizens of Los Angeles *(right)*. But beware, plagues are not just the stuff of fiction...

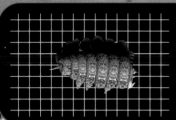

"**T**his is beyond me," gasped Edgar Hyde, PhD. "Whatever caused this, one thing is certain — we are dealing with something that is powerful and deadly. It must be found and destroyed at once."

Three days had passed since the pilots' tale reached the authorities. Hyde was part of a scientific team that had been rushed to the island.

Further inland, biologist Emma Barden picked her way through the twisted bodies, looking for clues. All were covered in strange bites. But no snake venom would have produced such horrible blisters. Then Barden thought she spotted something moving. Instinct told her to investigate.

She gagged in horror. Writhing weakly on the ground was a fat, green-gray maggot, its slimy skin gleaming dully. Bravely, she picked up the foul creature and dropped it in a jar. It couldn't be this...

The word "plague" is used to describe any disease which causes the deaths of many people at the same time. It can also mean any large-scale pestilence, such as a swarm of insects which destroy crops or people.

LET'S TWIST AGAIN

Myths and legends about plagues of creatures range from mysterious rains of frogs *(right)* to showers of crocodiles! Scientists believe these mysterious phenomena are caused by weather conditions such as tornados, whose twisting wind sucks the animals high into the air, dropping them only when the wind dies down.

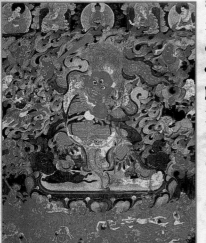

HEAVENS ABOVE!

Plagues have wreaked havoc since humankind began, and perhaps even longer. The first written evidence dates from about 2000 B.C. The ancient Babylonian poem *The Epic of Gilgamesh* (its hero Gilgamesh is shown *right*) refers to Irra, the vengeful god of pestilence.

Many other societies have sought to explain natural disasters as the actions of vengeful gods (such as the Tibetan Begtse, *above*). In the 14th century, a terrible plague known as the Black Death *(page 11)* was depicted as a demonic skeleton, stretching its horrible body over London. Many medieval Christians felt it to be an agent sent by God to teach the world a lesson.

As the scalpel slipped into the flesh of the maggot, a foul smell filled the laboratory. Barden and Hyde stepped backward in disgust. Nothing had prepared them for this.

Edgar yawned. They had stepped off the strato-shuttle and rushed to the laboratory. Barden hadn't even allowed him a cup of coffee before they got to work. Emma saw the yawn, and smiled. It was easy to forget the time when you were working on something this fascinating. "Let's have a look at this, and then we'll get something to eat," she said.

Silence fell as Barden and Hyde concentrated on the strange creature before them. They couldn't take their eyes off its oversized body, swollen with the blood of its last victim. Hyde's thoughts were far from his tired eyes or hungry stomach.

The lab was tightly sealed with thick glass panels to prevent deadly viruses from escaping. Nothing, not even a sound, could enter. Or so they thought...

Suddenly, the heavy doors shattered in a shower of glass. Two men burst in, dressed in airtight protective clothing. One threw a gas canister into the lab. Barden and Hyde sank to the floor, losing consciousness within seconds.

THE PLAGUES OF EGYPT

According to the biblical Book of Exodus, written in about 1000-500 B.C. but probably based on much older events, the Plagues of Egypt were called up by Moses to punish Egypt. Scientists are now trying to explain these plagues. Do they have a basis in fact?

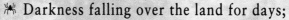

PESTILENTIAL PLAGUES

The Plagues of Egypt included:

✳ "Sores that break into pustules on Man and beast" – in fact, this was probably caused by an outbreak of measles or smallpox *(page 25)*.

✳ The Nile River flowing red with blood – this could have been the effect of a volcano bringing red earth to the surface of the river!

✳ Darkness falling over the land for days;

✳ Falling, burning soot;

✳ Scorching winds;

✳ Fiery hail in the sky – these last four events may all have been the after-effects of a recent volcanic eruption *(below right)*.

✳ A swarm of locusts *(left)* – this is now known to be fairly common in Africa *(page 15)*.

COME AGAIN?

Some experts believe that these terrible phenomena may have been caused by a comet *(top)* which passed so close to the Earth that it disrupted its gravity, thus causing changes in nature. They argue that this might even have been the cause of the biblical story of Moses' famous parting of the Red Sea!

"**Q**uick – grab the jar and let's get out of here." Chaos reigned as the thieves, protected from the deadly fumes by gas masks, searched frantically for their prize.

"Got it!" cried one, clutching the bottle in which several of the creatures squirmed. Alarms rang, but to no avail. The thieves ran past the guards, rendered powerless by the potent fumes of the gas. A hi-speed hoverbike could be heard zooming away into the night.

As the gas cleared, Hyde opened his eyes blearily. "What's ha..." His voice trailed off as he caught sight of Barden's horrified gaze. Pale and trembling, she was staring at the empty space where their precious specimen jar had been.

"E...Edgar," she whispered, "They're gone. GONE. Those things are out there. We don't even know what they are... or how to destroy them. What have we done?"

DARK DESTROYER

Of all the plagues in history, none was so feared, or so widespread, as bubonic plague, also known as the "Black Death" because black sores appeared on the skins of victims. First recorded in Athens in 430 B.C., its history is long and deadly.

A MEDIEVAL MALADY

The most famous outbreak of Black Death occurred in 14th-century Asia and Europe, killing up to 25 percent of the population (*above*). It continued to devastate Europe until the late 17th century.

"Plague doctors" wore protective clothing (their long beak was filled with antiseptic substances, *left*).

But the plague killed all those who caught it. Thousands were buried at a time – a few unlucky ones were buried alive! When their bodies were dug up, like that of Arnold Paole (*right*), the plague had turned their gums red and their skin pale. Because of this, stories of vampires were common.

TINY BUT DEADLY

The bubonic plague bacillus, *Yersinia pestis* (*left*), is carried by the fleas of black rats. It is thought to have originated in the Himalayas. As early humans migrated to Asia, the rats moved to these areas to find food. From there they spread to Europe, and the rest is history. The plague exists today, but now victims have a 50 percent chance of survival.

"Well done, my friends!" boomed Henry Chancellor. "Soon the world will be ours. But tonight we celebrate our success!" They all drank excessively.

Chancellor had assembled his team from the world's most feared and ruthless criminals — and his investment had already paid off. He grinned to himself as he watched them singing and cheering.

With the deadly beasts stolen from Barden's lab, he would hold the world hostage. Nothing would be denied him. From the bowels of Alpha City, he would control the future of the world.

The gang had broken into a rowdy dance. The alcohol had taken effect, and, as they reeled around the room, crashing into walls and furniture, no one noticed that the jar of specimens had cracked. The noise of the festivities stirred the sluggish creatures inside.

One by one, the slugs made the arduous climb up the glass sides of the jar, squeezing their revolting, deadly bodies out through the crack...

S W A R M !

Thousands of swarming creatures – everyone hates the idea... but we love to see them in movies. Perhaps the most famous swarm film is Alfred Hitchcock's 1963 movie *The Birds* which continues to terrify audiences with its scenes of killer bird attacks *(right)*.

BEE CAREFUL!

If you are afraid of spiders, then avoid the film *Arachnophobia* (1990) like the plague! It tells the story of the struggle by a doctor, a mad scientist, and an exterminator against an invading force of deadly spiders. But don't worry – it could never happen. Spiders usually work alone to hunt their prey. *The Swarm* (1978, *right*) featured an attack on a Texas town by a huge swarm of killer bees from Africa!

DEEP – AND DEADLY!

A spoof based on *Jaws* (1975), *Piranha* (1978, *left*) was a fairly silly film – an accident leads to the release of a mad doctor's people-munching piranhas. But it is true that piranhas can give you a nasty bite. Rumor has it that a school of piranhas can strip a human body to a skeleton in a few minutes...

Later that night, Chancellor's vast underground complex echoed with the drunken snores of his henchmen. Even the criminal mastermind himself was slumped over a table. All was still... or was it?

Many of the creatures had died as they crawled out of the jar, their strength sapped. But the others, though sluggish, had sought hiding places, such as the complex's oxygen supply pipes.

In an accommodation cave, Mitchell, one of Chancellor's thugs, was in a drunken sleep, unaware of the horror that was approaching him. He did not feel the weight of the fat grub as it dropped onto his arm. With a burst of energy, the ghastly creature sank its fearsome teeth into the soft flesh above Mitchell's elbow, and sucked out a few drops of blood.

It writhed horribly as it pierced another hole with its hollow, needlelike tail. A huge convulsion ripped through its body and a gleaming mass of tiny gray eggs poured into Mitchell's arm. He stirred, feeling the sting, and knocked the creature off the bed. Exhausted by its efforts, the grub died before it hit the floor.

BLIGHTS

Today, the world's most devastating pestilences are those which destroy crops *(below)*, thus ruining the livelihood of those who depend on them. Scientists are constantly developing ways of combating these terrible blights, but the forces of nature continue to thwart their efforts.

LETHAL LOCUSTS

The most feared insects in Africa and some parts of Asia are locusts *(above)*, which can ruin crop fields in an astonishingly short time. When large groups of locusts gather, they start to travel together in search of food. The swarms can contain up to 100 million insects covering an area over 3,500 miles across. And wherever they land, they feed. Another serious crop pest is the weevil *(right)*, the name given to many long-snouted beetles. These attack cotton fields, fruit, and seeds.

MUSHROOM MENACE?

A fungus is a plant which has no stem or roots and so has to live as a parasite on other plants. Mushrooms are the most well known... but there are thousands of others which can devastate crops, spreading rapidly by shedding their spores. In the Middle Ages, the fungus *Claviceps purpura* contaminated rye, causing an epidemic known as St. Anthony's Fire.

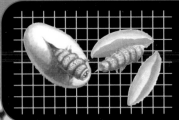

"**I**t is now 0600 hours. Time for the morning shift." The announcement was harsh, abrupt... and very, very loud. It tore through Mitchell's head like a foghorn.

He felt terrible. How much had he drunk the night before? Surely not that much. If he didn't get up, Chancellor would have him for breakfast. "Come on," he thought to himself, "You'll feel better once you've had something to eat."

But however much he tried, his eyes were shut fast. He put his hands to his face and, to his horror, felt huge, hard lumps all over his skin. "What the...?" he exclaimed, but his words died in his throat as a wave of hot, searing pain erupted through his body.

Panic-stricken, he sat up and felt his skin. The boils were covering his whole body, and the pain was increasing by the second. He tried to scream, but his throat was dry and only a strangled gargling noise escaped.

Mitchell scrambled around the room, fumbling wildly. He felt like he was being boiled alive. His hand fell upon the doorknob... but it was too late. With a final, silent scream, he fell to the floor.

SECRET THIEVES

While some pests are only too visible, others are doing their worst in hidden places – under the leaves on a forest floor, inside a tree's bark *(left),* in muddy waters, and even inside our bodies. High levels of human infection frequently occur in places with poor sanitation, as these parasites often lay their eggs in rotting food.

LURKING LEECHES

A babbling brook might look inviting – but be careful if you step into one! Leeches are wormlike parasites with a sucker at either end of their bodies. They use these to cling to their prey, then they bite the skin and suck out the blood *(right).* They can be detached by sprinkling them with salt or by burning them. Leeches were used as a cure for all sorts of illnesses for hundreds of years.

ENOUGH TO MAKE YOU "SQWORM!"

Helminths are a group of parasitic worms, which grow in and feed on humans and animals. More than 2 million people have roundworms at any one time! They can grow up to 18 inches long. Hookworms attach themselves to the intestines, and suck blood from the blood vessels. A tapeworm *(right)* fixes itself by its head to the intestines to feed – the whole creature can grow up to 30 feet long!

"Mitchell, where are you? It's 0800 hours and you're still asleep? You'd better be at your briefing in five minutes or you're a dead man. Do you hear me, Mitchell?... OK, I'm coming in."

"Crusher" Edmonds grasped the doorknob and tried to burst into the room. But the door was jammed. "Come on, Mitchell, stop playing around," barked Edmonds. "Unblock the door — that's an order."

Silence. Edmonds put his shoulder to the door and heaved. The air was filled with a putrid stench and a vile squelching noise. Mitchell's twisted, sore-covered body lay slumped behind the door. Thousands of glistening slugs oozed from beneath his skin, their deadly jaws working furiously. Edmonds screamed, and slipping on the seething mass of fat bugs, ran from the room as fast as he could. Unaffected by this interruption, the terrible creatures munched on.

Many creatures form swarms, but whatever the reason, millions of hungry beasts approaching at high speed is a pretty awesome sight – and dangerous too.

For many creatures, especially small ones, the swarming habit begins even before birth. Animals such as fish and turtles lay large numbers of eggs. In this way, some of their young will avoid attacks from larger predators and the species will survive.

PACK ATTACK

Ants (*right*) forage in large numbers for food to take back to their nests. By working as a team, they are able to carry pieces of food many times heavier than a single insect's body weight.

African army ants live in columns of up to a million members. While small workers travel in the center, large soldiers spread out at the sides of the column to pick up any creature that cannot sprint out of range. Lion cubs, wounded cattle, and pythons have all been devoured by these fearless hunters.

DANCING DANGER

Spiders tend to function alone but they have always presented a terrible threat. In the Middle Ages, in Italy it was believed that a person could cure a tarantula bite by dancing wildly. Today, the "Tarantella" is a popular dance!

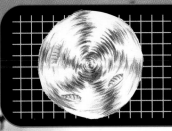

Two days later, Hyde and Barden looked on in terror as a sore-ridden Edmonds stood shaking before them. "I had to come," he stuttered, "for the sake of the planet."

In a trembling hand, he held a bag, filled with squirming grubs. "They k... killed one of us," he continued. "We torched most of them, but Chancellor was determined to keep some alive. The stupid fool got bitten. When he knew he was going to die, he flushed some into the sewers — they could be anywhere by now. I don't have long to live, but I beg you, you must find a way to stop them."

Edgar grabbed the bag — "Now, where's your complex?" But knowing he had just hours to live, Edmonds disapeared. Hearing his story, Barden realized with sickening horror that the grubs were out there, and multiplying at a terrifying rate...

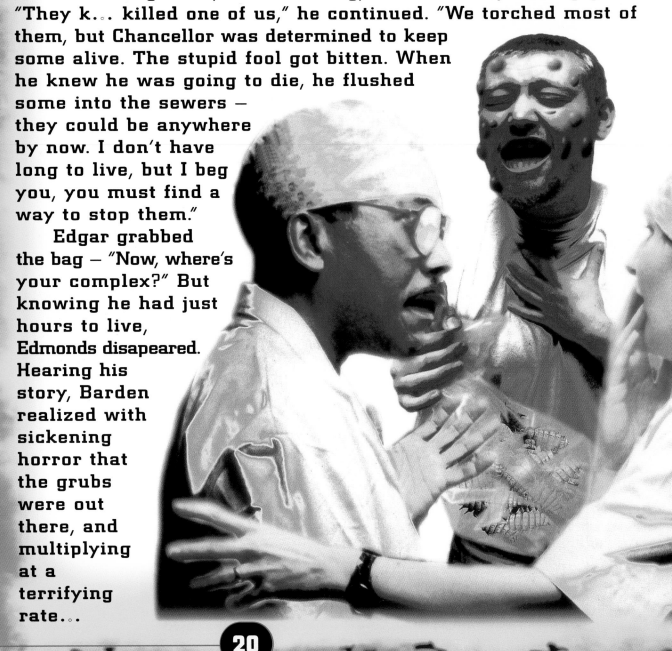

THE INVISIBLE ENEMY

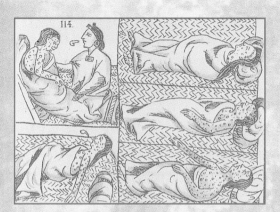

So tiny that they can be seen only with a microscope, bacteria and viruses *(right)* are responsible for some of history's most devastating natural disasters. When Spanish conquistadors invaded Central America in the 16th century, they carried smallpox and typhus viruses that killed perhaps a third of the Aztec population *(left)*.

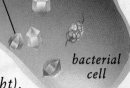

BATTLING BACILLI

Bacteria are single-celled organisms which reproduce rapidly by splitting. The body produces antibodies – substances which fight bacteria – but as they reproduce, some bacteria become resistant to these. Harmful bacteria thrive in places where there are no antibodies, such as in food. This is one reason why the bubonic plague bacillus was carried so quickly by flea-ridden rats *(left)*.

bacteriophage

VORACIOUS VIRUSES

Viruses are much smaller than bacteria, and like most bacteria, can live harmlessly alongside (or inside!) humans. Others cause diseases from a cold to mumps. Some viruses, known as bacteriophages *(right)*, even inhabit and kill bacteria. Viruses develop in living cells where they multiply rapidly. New viruses leave the cell, spreading to new areas *(right)*.

new viruses forming

bacterial cell

"This is an emergency news flash. The World Corporation has issued the following health warning. Do not leave your living quarters. Report any creature sightings immediately."

Barden felt that she and Hyde were in some way to blame for unleashing this army of monstrous maggots on the world. But even her quick warning to the Corporation could not prevent the nightmare that was about to descend on the citizens of Alpha City at a lightning speed. The slimy deadly creatures did not care who their victims were — men, women, and children, even animals — any being full of precious blood could be used as a breeding ground.

Health warnings blared from television, and loudspeakers, but to no avail. The creatures seemed to come from nowhere.

The horrible killers were sliming their way across Alpha City via the rats that lived in the vast sewer systems. Here, the damp, warm conditions suited them well, and the rats carried them secretly into their victims' homes.

The city officials of Alpha City offered a vast reward to anyone who could end this plague. Scientists all over the world worked night and day in their laboratories in an attempt to find a remedy that would rid Alpha of this creeping death.

SEEKING SOLUTIONS

Before the invention of the microscope, which allowed people to look at otherwise invisible bacteria and viruses, no one knew what caused disease. Theories came and went. Some were based on scientific knowledge; others were founded in magic and superstition.

IN GOOD HUMOR

For centuries, scientists were influenced by the Greek physician Hippocrates (460–380 B.C.), and his theory of humors *(right)*. According to him, the "humors" – the body's four basic fluids (blood, phlegm, and yellow and black bile) represented the earth's four elements (water, earth, fire, and air).

An imbalance in the humors could cause disease or mood swings. A popular "cure" was bleeding (some bleeding tools are shown *top right)*. It was thought that by taking out some blood, the body would be rid of the excess "bad" humor *(top left)*!

LEEUWENHOEKS' LENSES

In 1674, Dutch inventor Anton van Leeuwenhoek (1632–1723) used the first microscope *(left)* to study tiny "animalcules... moving in the most delightful manner" (his drawings are shown *below)*. Only now did scientists begin to think that disease could be caused by tiny organisms. Leeuwenhoek did not realize it, but he was looking at bacteria (viruses were too tiny to be seen). At last, we could see our invisible enemies, and begin to fight back.

"**I**t stinks in here. This had better be worth it — if we don't win that money, I'll feed you to the slugs." The sewers echoed with the sound of creature seekers armed with powerful laser

Three weeks had passed, and the plague was getting worse every day. The reward offered by the city officials had only attracted a motley crew of bounty hunters, often more deadly than the insects themselves.

By day and night, they roamed the streets, splashed through the drains, and ransacked houses, terrifying the already weary residents. Armed with a variety of weapons, they managed to kill some insects — but possessed by greed, they ruthlessly killed thousands of innocent citizens.

For all their efforts, the grub population continued to rise. No one could have known that there were many more to come, growing secretly inside the city's countless sewer rats. They were just waiting for the right moment to burst out in their

THE TERRIBLE POX

The dreaded disease of smallpox was used in the first case of biological warfare – it was deliberately spread by European settlers to wipe out the indigenous peoples of the "New World." Thanks to the work of one man, today it has been almost wiped out.

THE POX...

Smallpox attacked quickly, and by the late 18th century, it had killed one person in ten in Europe. It began with pains, followed a day later by fever, and then a rash and sores. If patients survived, they might be left blind or with pockmarked skin *(left)*. No one was safe: In 1774, smallpox killed King Louis XV of France.

THE PIONEER...

English surgeon Edward Jenner had treated many cases of cowpox. He noticed that once a person had this mild disease, he or she was unlikely to catch smallpox. In 1796, he scratched James Phipps's arm with a scalpel covered in cowpox. He then injected him with smallpox itself, with no effect! Jenner became famous, but was also ridiculed in cartoons *(top)*, claiming that his vaccination would turn people into cows!

AND THE PIPER

Some people believe the story of the Pied Piper of Hameln *(right)* is connected to plagues. The rats that he leads out of the city represent the diseases that swept the towns of medieval Germany.

"WHOOSH! Out of the city's sewers burst a seething mass of gleaming grubs, their deadly jaws snapping wildly. Like a torrent of filthy slime, they swept through the city streets.

People in their way were engulfed in an instant, never to be seen again. Even those in their homes were not safe — thousands of creatures poured out of faucets and water tanks, filling a room in seconds.

Pandemonium broke out, as the desperate citizens tried to flee the city. They leaped into hover cars and trains, or ran for their lives. Thousands died in the chaos; those who made it would have to survive the barren lands outside the city walls. A few managed to board strato-shuttles and escape the city for a new life elsewhere. Those who stayed, hid, cowering in the tallest buildings where the grubs did not go. Who could save them?

From the window of the lab, Barden saw the terrible scenes outside. "This is all my fault," she wept. "This is no time for that," snapped Hyde. "How dare y..." stuttered Emma, red with rage.

But her colleague bravely ignored her protestations. "We have to keep going until we find a way to rid Alpha of these hideous creatures. Emma, only you can find the answer!"

INSECT CARRIERS

Some of the most deadly diseases have been carried across the world by insects like the mosquito or tsetse fly. For instance, the slave trade took mosquitoes infected with yellow fever from Africa to the Americas.

A WIDESPREAD PEST

Mosquitoes are among the world's greatest carriers of disease. The viruses of malaria and yellow fever affect millions of people every year, often with fatal consequences. Malaria is spread by mosquitoes sucking infected blood from one victim and passing it to another.

Only female mosquitoes bite, because the blood of their victims helps their eggs to develop. When they bite, they stab through our skin with six needlelike parts called stylets. Then saliva flows into the wound to help the blood flow. Most of us are allergic to this saliva, so an itchy welt called a "mosquito bite" forms on our skin.

THE SLEEPING DISEASE

Sleeping sickness is spread by the tsetse fly *(left)*, which carries infected parasites called trypanosomes in its stomach. When the fly bites an animal, these wormlike creatures travel via the fly's saliva into the victim's bloodstream.

19th-century European explorers were forced to rely on African bearers because all the horses they took with them died from the disease *(top)*.

"**E**dgar, get some sleep. We've been working for four days now and, if I may say so, you look terrible." Emma had forgiven Hyde for his sharp, but wise, words.

Hyde yawned and stretched out his arms, looking forward to a nice long sleep. But as he did so, his hand swung into a jar of the slugs, sending it flying. It landed in a nearby specimen case, full of large, leafy plants.

"Carlo's experiment!" groaned Barden. "Those plants are rare and he won't let anyone near them! Quick, get them out of the case!" Hyde rushed over to the cabinet... and gasped in amazement.

The creatures were munching away at the leaves — but as they did so, their bodies were becoming wrinkled and dry. Seconds later, they were writhing in agony, and within a minute they lay dead on the bottom of the case.

Could these rare plants save the world from the killer slugs? "Eureka!" shouted Hyde, jumping for joy. Emma tried to disguise her mounting hope from her colleague. "I know this looks encouraging, Edgar, but we should test this out properly — just to be sure."

INFECTION CONTROL

Started by Leeuwenhoek's discovery of "animalcules" *(page 23)*, microbiology (the study of microbes) has helped to solve many puzzles in the mystery world of disease. It was the work of Louis Pasteur, a 19th-century French chemist, that made this possible.

THE POWER OF THE MICROBE

Diseases like cholera continued to devastate communities well into the 19th century. The film *The Horseman on the Roof* (1996, *bottom*) highlights how terrified crowds still believed that supernatural forces were responsible. Pasteur's exhaustive experiments in the 1870s *(right)* proved that micro-organisms affected the world around them and that they could reproduce. Although Pasteur had not yet discovered viruses, he realized that some diseases must be caused by organisms even smaller than bacteria.

OUR LITTLE FRIENDS

In the 1930s, the electron microscope finally allowed scientists to see viruses. Since then, the study of microbes has advanced at an astonishing speed, giving

doctors the power to control many diseases (including cholera). Scientists now use harmless microbes to help rather than harm humans. Fungi such as penicillin produce antibodies to destroy bacteria, sometimes by locking onto the bacteria's surface *(above left)*. Other organisms are used to break down harmful substances in drinking water.

 **T**hat night was filled with death — but this time it was the creatures that writhed in agony as their bodies were destroyed by the plant extract. Barden and Hyde felt sure that this was the cure.

Barden was using the plants to create a powerful poison. "We must use it sparingly. These plants are rare — if we run out it would be disastrous." Several hours later came a triumphant cry: "I've done it! One drop of this should kill a grub in seconds."

"Those maggots won't know what's hit 'em," shouted Hyde eagerly.

"We must make sure that the poison won't kill humans," Barden stated firmly. Before Edgar could protest, she had rashly downed an entire cup of the plant extract. Suddenly she staggered and clutched her stomach in agony. Hyde rushed to help her. "Emma? Emma, are you all right?"

"That stuff is disgusting!" laughed Emma — so she did have a sense of humor, after all! Hyde tried not be angry. But this was no time for emotions.

The citizens of Alpha City were on a mission — to search for the rare plant.

NASTY BY NATURE

Many creatures carry diseases that can be transmitted easily to humans. Some, like bats *(right)*, have become immune to the diseases they carry. Scientists are now exploring ways of genetically treating plants *(bottom left)* to make them immune to any pests or plagues which may destroy them.

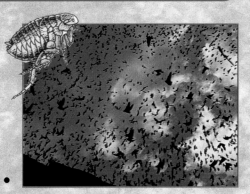

● ●

HIGH-JUMPING HORRORS

Fleas *(left)* carry both typhus and bubonic plague, but unlike their human victims, they can fight both viruses and expel them from their bodies. The flea's strong legs help it to glide quickly through the hairs on the body of its host, and then it uses its beak to puncture the victim's skin. To find a human flea, try looking in the folds of your clothing. But watch out – it may only be 0.1 inch long but it can jump over 12 inches!

● ●

BARKING MAD

One of the most terrifying diseases is rabies, carried by dogs *(right)*, raccoons, and the vampire bats of South America. If bitten by a rabid animal, the victim will foam at the mouth, losing huge amounts of fluid – yet even a tiny amount of water can paralyse them. Death usually occurs after four to five days. In 1885, however, Louis Pasteur managed to develop a vaccine that helped to protect people against the disease.

"**H**igh Command to all armed forces. Every available unit will proceed at once to collect specimens of the plant *Spongifora bulbosa*. This is priority 9 command. Scramble. Scramble."

Barden supervised the massive operation as the production of the poison began. Huge drums spun, pressing out the precious juices from the plants. Load after load of plants arrived at all hours, to be processed and tested.

Yet within two days the supplies dwindled, then stopped altogether. "There are no more plants!" Edgar cried, "And we only have a third of the poison we need!"

"We'll have to dilute it... and hope," said Barden. When the mixing was done, she let a drop fall onto one of the creatures. Silence fell. As the creature's body contorted, shriveling up lifelessly, a great cheer arose in the lab, a cheer of joy and relief.

NEW VACCINES

Though the new science of microbiology made a huge difference in the battle against disease, the fight was by no means over in the 20th century.

• •

VACCINE VICTORY

The work of Dr. Jonas Salk *(right)* contributed greatly to the health of the 20th-century world. He contributed greatly to the development of an

influenza vaccine. Most people have had the "flu" at some time, and it usually goes away after a day or two. But influenza has caused some of the deadliest plagues. In the epidemic of 1918–1919, up to 22 million people died. People tried many contraptions to avoid catching it *(left)*.

Then, in 1955, Salk's discovery of the vaccine against the polio virus made him a hero. This deadly virus was passed in contaminated drinking water and severely affected the nervous system. Today, polio has almost disappeared from developed countries.

• •

MAKING IT UP

As plagues continue to haunt the world, writers and filmmakers have dreamed up all kinds of new pestilences. In *Twelve Monkeys* (1996), an unknown virus has devastated the planet Earth, and its survivors must live underground. The hero travels back in time to stop the virus spreading *(right)*!

"This is it, folks - our last chance. Give it all you've got. Remember, the people of Alpha City are depending on you. Good luck." A handful of pilots had the life of millions in their hands.

With an earth-shattering roar, a squadron of spraying craft burst from the vast underground hangar at Alpha City's military airport. They blasted off in all directions, to rid the city of its terrible affliction. Meanwhile, thousands of soldiers swarmed into the sewers, armed with spray guns filled with the poison. Once it got into the water, it would destroy even those killer grubs growing in rat hosts.

Once again, the city was a scene of panic - but now it was the slugs that were fleeing for their lives. The sprayers were merciless, engulfing the whole city in a thick veil of bright green plant extract that sparkled in the air as it caught the sun's dying rays. Sensing the danger of this deadly rain, the maggots slithered desperately across the city — but there was no escape.

As you have seen, plagues are still a terrifying reality even in a world of medical wizardry and hi-tech procedures. Some are sealed off from the world; some have only just appeared on our planet; and a few are even used in warfare, in a terrible modern development...

THE HI-SECURITY POX

Thanks to a global effort in the 20th century, no one in the world now has smallpox, and the virus has also been wiped out from the environment. But scientists are unwilling to let it disappear completely, in case it is ever needed for future research. So the world's last surviving smallpox viruses are kept in sealed laboratories in the Russian and U.S. Centers for Disease Control (*above*). The security at both labs is intense – smallpox must never plague our planet again.

OUTBREAK

In 1973, a Zairean hospital reported an outbreak of a strange disease which caused severe bleeding, diarrhea, and vomiting. Samples of the strange virus were sent to hi-security laboratories; the mysterious and deadly virus (*above*) was named Ebola.

PREPARED FOR PLAGUE

Military personnel (*right*) are now trained to deal with the release of deadly viruses of bacteria by an enemy power. The consequences of germ warfare are devastating, but the threat is frighteningly real.

Within minutes, a change could be seen in the behavior of the creatures. They stopped their attempts to escape, and as the poison got to work, they twisted and turned like leaves in the wind.

One by one, the grubs shriveled up and wrinkled. Their fat bodies burst, letting forth a torrent of pus and blood, both their own and that of their hapless victims.

The streets were covered with dying creatures, and the stench was unbearable — a hideous, rotten smell that intensified as the minutes passed and more and more maggots perished. The drains became clogged up with the creatures as they died in their millions.

For what seemed like an eternity, the beleaguered citizens of Alpha City watched the gruesome spectacle from tower blocks and walkways. But by nightfall, everything was still once more.

There had been a massive loss of life... but the city was safe at last.

Plagues and pestilence have allowed filmmakers to go wild! Movies have covered every possible plague situation, some with humor, others with horror...

✹ *The Masque of the Red Death* (1964), was genuinely chilling. Based on an Edgar Allen Poe short story, the film recounts how a 14th-century count refuses to let local villagers shelter from a plague raging outside his castle. But in the end, he catches the plague himself (*below left*)!

✹ *Outbreak,* (1995, *above center*) is a frightening contemporary tale about a lethal virus that escapes from a research laboratory (*page 35*) and is spread by an infected monkey bought as a pet.

✹ *Rabid* (1977, *right*) presented a bleak vision of a future world where people became infected with a rabies-like disease which transformed them into foaming murderous animals.

✹ *Monty Python and the Holy Grail,* (1974, *above right*) made a joke of medieval life, including a scene where a gang of Black Death collectors take people even though they're still alive – in fact, not that far from the truth (*page 11*)!

"Three cheers for Barden and Hyde, saviors of Alpha City!" The roar of the crowd echoed across the city as Edgar and Emma mounted the steps of the World Corporation Building to collect their medals from the council of city officials.

A week had passed since the destruction of the maggots. The survivors had worked hard to clean the streets and to bury and honor the dead. Outside the city walls, huge bonfires, fueled by the massed bodies of dead grubs, burned with eerie, green flames. The creatures were gone forever, and Alpha City was eager to forget the devastation.

Even in the midst of the adoring crowd, Emma felt guilty. If only she had acted sooner, thousands of people could have been saved. "Stop that right now," came a voice in her ear. "I know what you're thinking," said Edgar, "and you mustn't. You saved all of these people and that's what counts." Emma smiled, and gave the crowd another wave.

Stephanie Fell smiled as she watched her on the television. "I hope I can be like her when I grow up," she whispered. "What do you think, Caspar?" The cat arched and stretched on her lap. He was feeling very strange. He turned around and lay down to lick one of the large, itchy boils that were appearing on his body...

GERM TERMS

Antibody – A chemical produced by white blood cells in the body, to combat the harmful effects of a "foreign" body such as a bacterium or virus.

Bacillus – A disease-causing bacterium.

Bacterium (plural **Bacteria**) – A single-celled microscopic organism which reproduces rapidly, by splitting into two. Some bacteria cause diseases in plants and animals.

Blight – A disease causing the withering of crops and plants.

Epidemic – A disease that attacks large numbers of people in one place over a short period of time.

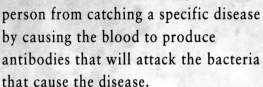

Immune – This means that a person will not catch a specific disease, because the person's body has a natural resistance to the disease, or because he or she has been vaccinated against it.

Microbes – Also known as micro-organisms, these are microscopic living things or organisms, including some fungi, bacteria, and viruses, which often cause diseases.

Microscopic – So tiny that it can only be seen with a microscope, an instrument for magnifying minute objects.

Organism – A living structure that can reproduce itself.

Parasite – An organism that lives and feeds off another, without giving anything good back in return.

Pestilence – A plague, either a disease or a swarm of pests e.g. locusts.

Phenomenon – A remarkable thing or event.

Vaccine – A drug which prevents a person from catching a specific disease by causing the blood to produce antibodies that will attack the bacteria that cause the disease.

Virus – A microscopic organism that only lives in a cell of another living thing. Some viruses infect humans with diseases such as influenza or measles. Others infect animals or plants or attack other bacteria. Viruses produce disease by damaging the cells of an organism.

INDEX

PHOTOCREDITS

Abbreviations; t – top, m – middle, b – bottom, r – right, l – left
Pages 4, 31b, & 35m & b – Frank Spooner Pictures; 5 & 37m – Warner Bros. Courtesy Kobal; 7 – Ancient Art & Architecture Collection; 8t, 28t, 32t, & 39 – Glaxo Holdings plc; 9 & 15t Solution Pictures; 10t, l2t, 15m, & 22t – Roger Vlitos; 11t, 25t & m, & 29m – Mary Evans Picture Library; 11b, 15b, 27b, & 35t – Science Photo Library; 13 all & 37r – Ronald Grant Archive; 14t, 17m, 19, & 33t – Bruce Coleman Collection; 21t, 23 both, 25b, & 31t – AKG London Hachette/France; 2 – C.E.C. courtesy Kobal; 31b – Hulton Getty Collection; 37l – A.I.P. courtesy Kobal; 37b – New World courtesy Kobal.